Your
Futuristic
Future

YOUR FUTURISTIC FUTURE

Project 99999+99999=1

Raymond Samora

To order additional copies of this book, contact:
Xlibris LLC
1-888-795-4274
www.Xlibris.com
Orders@Xlibris.com
626175

Introduction

It was not what RJ Sumner wanted out of life. Living his life out naturally was not intended on these basics. RJ wants to welcome everybody in the world to his new project—project 99999 + 99999 = 1. For everybody that chooses to, there are a lot of ways to improve your simple life. RJ project 99999

+ 99999 = 1 would turn the whole world around and make life better for everybody without any hassles. You see, RJ has been studying computer science. Ever since he got old enough to type, his first words typed into the computer were *science for the future*. He has read hundreds of books on computer science. Now he's one of the best scientists in the world, working on his family DNA and capturing their memories' DNA for further development. He is going to be able to make everybody in the world very intelligent. But it is going to cost you. But RJ Sumner will absolutely guarantee advancement his project, with new levels of the human brain and unlimited goals. He can guarantee that you will never be going back to the way you were living before. RJ, mastering his project, will improve your everyday living quality. This is a category in itself that will bring your consciousness to an upper level with your new developed brain. For anybody that chooses to, it will end sadness and sickness in your life, and you will become highly intelligent for eternity. Here are some examples that you will be able to experience: like it programs your brain to wake you up at any time you wish without a sound. Nobody will be able to outsmart each other, nor will your brain ever get lazy nor will anybody be able to murder you. What can be accomplished is endless.

RJ Sumner is a male in his early thirties, very handsome and very intelligent, and he attended the University of Hartford. The Bachelor of Science in Computer Science is designed to prepare a futuristic project, project 99999 + 99999 = 1, your futuristic future. If only we could utilize everybody's brain to its full capacity. Learning outcomes for a BS in computer science, you either got it or you don't. RJ is a computer scientist now. He is married to a very wonderful and beautiful wife, and her name is Cassie, along with their two kids, a boy and a girl ages ten and eight years old. They make a nice living in the beautiful city of Albuquerque, New Mexico. RJ works at the Sandia Labs in Albuquerque, and his wife Cassie is an RN and works at the Veterans Hospital, in the sleep apnea clinic on the sixth floor. The teaching of the word of God in this matter is absolutely constant. Married couples are to procreate indiscriminately and without the most unfortunate that would ever happen. Less common are examples of men and women who have striven to sustain a self-process that is inclusively international in attitude and behavior.

For the same and for good reason, it's going to happen, and RJ is going change it—the behavior and everybody's way of thinking. RJ Sumner's nation, culture, and society exert tremendous influence on each and everyone, how we live our lives, structuring our values, becoming engineers, our view of the world, and having full capacity of our mind and patterning our responses to experience computer science. The way information is grouped into a file is entirely up to how it is designed, which can become very time-consuming if there are many files to safeguard. It's better to work in codes. In his project $99999 + 99999 = 1$, RJ has to work with codes; no way around it. You have to be very precise with codes in this field. Human beings cannot hold themselves apart from some form of cultural influence. No one culture is free without a cause. Yet the conditions of contemporary history are in such a way that we may now be on the threshold of a new kind of you that wants to become one, a new person who is socially and psychologically beyond a product of the interweaving of cultures in the twenty-first century.

Your brain's wireless transmission is free. Your birth mind has no innate ideas; it is blank. RJ would like to change that so that infants will be able to communicate with you. It contains also a record of many of the reflections that afterward took shape in the making. It refers to the ability of a microprocessor to apparently process several tasks simultaneously inside the human mind—a chance of a lifetime, you get to make a difference in your short life. One trick is to remember your past. That will really help you cope in life in a better, more relaxing way. They say that the hand is quicker than the eyes. Our minds are set in a way that you are in control of you. We are stuck in them old ways of thinking—that's what's wrong with the human mind nowadays. It needs to be programmed differently. RJ says that to see what's wrong with that, we must avoid one naive trap. Just as one person learns to rearrange his mind and building blocks in clever ways, another person might. Such programs automatically apply rules whenever they're needed, so the facts are there.

Now let's face the other simple fact: our notions of the human mind are just as primitive. RJ will be working on the human mind, to have it programmed so we can get away from that old way of functioning. Truly slickly and furiously, mystically wired. We are designed to make connections to the unknown. RJ is gonna put the world away for a minute, pretending he's going to start a new life without an earth. So he won't have an earth to survive. Because it's not what the world takes away from you that counts; it's what you do with what you have left. I needed this more than you can imagine, and I need it now; it can show the human spirit in all its glory, where you can be down. We can train the computer program to recognize the patterns from millions of codes that a human have to go through. Our mind often plays tricks on us, and that is one of the key ones to be aware of. See how the human brain works using our interactive exhibit guide. Here are just a few of the wonderful things that brain balance has done for RJ Sumner. And he's very pleased to tell you that he's only two years into his project and he got it programmed to work temporarily now. RJ's invention will take roots soon. RJ's brains only weighs about three pounds, yet the greedy scientist uses between 20 percent and 25 percent of his brain. Getting the audio program tuned will take extra time. "I know what to do, so why don't I do it?" he said. But a hundred percent operating brain is what RJ is aiming for, and he wants full capacity of his brain; that is where his real future life begins.

Albuquerque, New Mexico, is such a wonderful city to live in.

They got one of most beautiful sunsets you ever see. And Albuquerque got surrounding mountains too, along with some nice sun-shining days. A reflection of reality that's needed to be addressed in building a sustainable future life for him and his whole family. Progressive poets prefer to look forward into the distant future that nobody has ever experienced before. RJ works very hard in this very high-security lab, and RJ has learned a lot at this Sandia Labs.

It's a government multiprogram engineering and science laboratory operated by Sandia Corporation for the US Department of Energy. RJ got to have a tight lid on his mouth. And RJ does. He knows the consequences. So he's staying away from the leaking out of information from the Sandia Labs.

Today, communication is essential to successful business operations, and the technology of the twenty-first century has become completely integrated into a business. And that's what RJ is looking forward to. In the ongoing debate as to whether communication technology is changing how we operate as human beings, there is one constant message: change is coming, for the deceased and for the living. And no more cemeteries to keep burying bodies. RJ is trying to change how we look at our past lives and change the future in a very new way. With good technology at hand, we can find a way to communicate with your loved ones after they have passed away. That's what's RJ is looking for—a good break.

There are many ways to back up files. Most computer systems provide utility programs to assist in the backup process, which can become very time-consuming. To figure out a way to be able to communicate with the deceased in a split second, with this new technology available, RJ can make it happen. You see, RJ has been having dreams about his wife's and kids' disappearance. And it's getting to him. After-death communication essentially confirms that life and love transcends death. It's a distinct feeling that your loved one is nearby, though he or she can't be seen. When you have two-way communication, it's usually by telepathy, which is the only way to communicate, and that's all in the present. This is the only resource we got at the present time. But with RJ's project 99999+99999= 1, it will be changed in the near future.

The nightmares force him to kick, move, and get up and walk around. The unpleasant nightmares, it's very important to RJ. And he's determined to know what's causing his nightmares. He's not sure if it's lack of oxygen to his brain. But with all this technology around, RJ has been so determined and willing to risk everything to get to the bottom of all these nightmares. And it's all about his family and dreaming of losing them in an airplane crash. RJ is working on a project that he has been working on for about eight years. He knows it is going to take time and money to be able to store his entire family inside a memory computer chip, to be able to communicate with them in case he'll lose them in an airplane crash according to the nightmares.

It's mid-May 2030. And school is out for the summer. And the kids are very happy, and they can hardly wait to start their swimming lessons. RJ is so happy for them. It's hard for RJ to keep up with the kids, especially when he doesn't get enough sleep. RJ mentions to his wife that he has to go see a doctor. And his wife looks at him with a very serious look.

She says, "It's about the nightmares."

RJ responds to his wife, with a smile and with a little worried look on his face, "Yep." RJ is very concerned. RJ mentions to his adorable wife, "When are you planning your trip overseas to go visit your grandmothers? You haven't seen her in two years."

Cassie says, "You are so right. I will make reservations on Monday, RJ. I know, RJ. You can't come with us because of your works. But I want to let you know that I love so very much."

RJ says to his wife, "I love you too, with all of my loving heart too, baby. We still got three months before you all fly overseas. So let's have fun with the kids all summer. Next two weeks, Cassie, I will be flying to Nevada, to Area 51. You know the rules, Cassie, that I can't say anything about anything about what's going on in my jobs. Because it's all confidential . . ."

"Yes, RJ," says Cassie. Cassie asks when he is getting back from Nevada.

"In about seven days." RJ wants to take a short trip to Fort Sumner, New Mexico, to go see the history of Billy the Kid and see where he is buried. "Oh, another thing that I heard is that there is a veteran in Fort Sumner who built a veteran memorial rest area ten miles north of Fort Sumner, New Mexico, on US 84 and Junction 203. And I hear that this special rest area, it's of one of the first and only veteran memorial rest area throughout the state of New Mexico. How cool is that?" RJ says. "I am sure that all veterans really like this veteran memorial rest area, for creating this special rest area for all veterans. Sure like to meet him," RJ says.

"After we get back from Fort Sumner, I have to finish my own personal labs," RJ says to his wife. "I will be going to my doctor appointment tomorrow. So wish me well," says RJ.

Cassie responds in a very sweet way as usual, "Yes, baby, I wish you the best."

RJ goes through his doctor appointment, and everything seems all right except for one thing. The doctor said, "It seems like you have symptoms of sleep apnea. I am setting you up with the sleep apnea testing at the VA hospital called a polysomnography."

Three weeks went by, and now RJ is back from Area 51 and is getting ready for his sleep apnea test. It is a test that is required to monitor sleep apnea; you may have a split-night sleep study.

During the first half of the night, the technician records your sleep patterns. You have to stay overnight to complete the test. And it will take a few days to complete the diagnosis.

Another week went by. RJ got the news, and it didn't look good. Yes, RJ was diagnosed with sleep apnea. Yes, RJ was disappointed for sure. Cassie took RJ's hand to calm him down.

"It's going to be all right, RJ," says Cassie. "Learn what causes it and how it's diagnosed and what you can do to help yourself and others with this disease. But frequent, loud snoring may be a sign of sleep apnea . . ."

That sounds like RJ.

"For sure it's a common thing. A person's sleep is needed to be energetic, mentally sharp, and productive the next day. You may be one and become one candidate for a sleep study, and you should see your doctor immediately."

A breathing aspirator will be issued to RJ to help him get the oxygen he needs to stay alive.

A month later, RJ is feeling more energetic than ever. RJ describes to his wife how the test went and how they did a general monitoring of his sleep and a variety of body functions during sleep, including breathing patterns along with oxygen levels in the blood, heart rhythms, and limb movements. RJ is intrigued how technology works. So now RJ wants to invent a way that he can capture and store a person's brain waves and store them into a computer chip so we can be able to communicate with one another without a human body being present. RJ believes that if he can make his project work, then he can live forever with his whole family and others that choose to.

"Another thing that I have to do, Cassie, is to store all of our DNAs separately. You don't want to cross someone else's DNA. I will try to get the labs up and going before you and the kids leave on your trip overseas." RJ has learned a lot of good things and stored a lot of information in codes that it needed.

RJ is having his sleep apnea test done on him. It is capturing some parts of his brain waves, but not all of it. He's sure he can capture the whole brain DNA of a person and store into a computer chip. Deep brain stimulation (DBS) is a surgical treatment that uses a device called a neurostimulator.

The extension wire connects the lead to the neurostimulator. But it will make contact and transmit the recorded brain waves to a receiver. Later you can transmit the brain waves into a computer chip. You have to make sure you are working with codes. If you don't know, you will never find your way back to start all over again. On the other hand, transmitting female brain waves needs more wiring. The male neural connections in a man's brain below are less complicated.

Women, on the other hand, have more wiring between the right and left female brain waves, which is another issue.

Cassie says to RJ, "Your project 99999 + 99999 = 1 has really gotten very interesting. Why are you teaching me your project 99999 + 99999 = 1?"

RJ says to Cassie, "You may have to use this project someday . . ."

"Thanks, RJ," says Cassie, not knowing that she would have to use this information in the near future, that the stored information will stick to her brain forever.

RJ asks Cassie, "Do you know why females need more wiring to capture their brain waves?"

Cassie says, "No."

"I want to explain to you, my sweet wife, Cassie. Females have to be wired differently because they have to give life to another human inside their bodies," RJ says. "In many ways, a lot of humans' brain can live for eternity. Think about it, Cassie my love.

Without electricity, you wouldn't be reading this article right now. And its protons have a positive charge, neutrons have a neutral charge, and electrons have a say-so on how your brain operates." RJ feels confident he can do it. Along with their DNA stored. "Cassie, you have to have confidence in me," RJ says. "By the way, Cassie there are ways for you to have been flummoxed, struggling to connect the five-dozen wires to my head." From RJ's textbook, it's the correct way from his design pattern. "That needed to be secretly coded . . . and no buts or ifs about it. Cassie, you have to know all of these codes to be able to use them, in case emergencies show up. This project $99999 + 99999 = 1$ is all for us, Cassie, so we can be able to visit and see the entire universe plus more exploring and having more fun than you ever imagine."

By now, everything is on hold because his wife wants to have a little fun and talk about the kids, that it's time to buy them some summer clothing.

"Sure," he says, "we go do it tomorrow."

Cassie asks RJ, "What's the movie all about that you telling about the other day, RJ?"

"The name of the movie is *50 to 1*," RJ says. "It's all about a horse owner out of Roswell, NM, who drives himself and his horse to the state of Kentucky to enter his horse into the Kentucky Derby. It's an event that takes place every year.

I heard it's a good movie," says RJ. RJ asks Cassie, "What are we having for supper?"

Cassie says, "How about tacos? And let's call it a taco day."

"That sounds pretty cool to me. Thanks, honey," says RJ. "Personally, Cassie, I wouldn't know what to do without you—my wife—and the kids. You all are my life and my destiny, Cassie. You all are so wonderful to me.

"Sleep apnea usually is a chronic [ongoing] condition that disrupts your sleep. When your breathing pauses or becomes shallow, you'll often move out of a sleep because your brain is starving for oxygen. Having sleep apnea has no options unless you take care of it medically. The point that I am getting across to you is that I had a sleep studies done, wires attached to my head and some to my chest, and wires attached to sensors transmitting the data to a computer in another room. I am hoping that project 99999 + 99999 = 1 can take place soon, for the benefit of the people and for us too. Being able to transmit stored memory into computer chips, for those people that choose to, so that they can live forever inside computer chips. I am sure it can be done. If one of your love ones happens to die, you are going to be able to communicate with that loved one—that's if you pay to have your DNA memory stored. Wouldn't it make you feel better, Cassie, that you are going to be able to do that? I am sure it's going to happen,

Cassie, for a price for sure," RJ says. "Our brains' wiring makes us who we are . . . of our brains' neuronal connections, the totality of how we are wired together. The purpose of RJ project $99999 + 99999 = 1$ is to capture and program the brain in several steps into further places that the brain has never been. No more burials with my invention. You may think that I am off just a little bit. But there's no limitation for the human mind. Technology is here to stay, so let's put it to use.

Why fill up the cemeteries with more dead bodies when you can capture someone's memories? Just think for a minute, Cassie. What I am trying to explain to you, honey, for just a second, is it is better to communicate with that person on the computer than visiting and taking flowers to a lonely cemetery. I am sure that Mr. Albert Einstein would have agreed with me and would've loved my idea. Being without beginning or end, existing outside of time. See synonyms of *infinite.* And continuing without interruption, or *perpetual.* RJ will show the whole world."

RJ's wife is full of love and excitement and is hugging and kissing her husband.

"Cassie, let me tell you something. Remember when I was having all of those nightmares?"

"Yes," says Cassie.

"My brain would stop sending messages to my lungs, and I couldn't breathe. It was like I was dead. But in way, I wasn't."

The mind keeps going until he got deeper inside his brain. Imaging with multiphoton microscopy, elucidating how the brain works is a grand challenge within RJ the scientist. It's a very brilliant way to know that his brain can rely on all those secret codes. Practically this is where RJ's been getting all his brilliant ideas. It's from having sleep apnea.

"Cassie, all this happened to me, and all of the nightmares and sleep apnea has helped me a lot . . . it all happens for a good reason," RJ says. "Let me tell you something, Cassie. I am into something good here with my project 99999 + 99999 = 1. For people that choose to, they will have a very good chance of reliving their lives again. That's what it comes down to. Eventually your life will come to end naturally. It's like a second-life policy on your loved ones. You know what I mean, Cassie, your first life will come to an end naturally. Cassie, I'm set up with my lab now, and all my education and experience on this field and being a computer scientist is paying off. A scientist who has acquired knowledge of computer science, the study of the theoretical foundations of information and computation, he should be able to patent this project, Cassie.

"I am taking the next week off to be with you all before you all take off on your trips. I will be working on the concept of an invention into a working device that is not always swift or direct, but I can work around the government codes that are needed in my project," says RJ. "With a good invention on hand, you'll be able to make a lot of money. It may also become more useful after time."

RJ says that he got confidence that his invention will work, like what the song says. RJ is always singing. You need time and more loving to perfect it.

Cassie says, "Honey, I wish you the best on your science project

99999 + 99999 = 1. You have always been so futuristic since I've known you. I am so proud of you, RJ."

RJ says to his wife, Cassie, "Thanks a lot, honey, so I'm lucky to have you forever and never getting old, thanks to RJ project 99999 + 99999 = 1." RJ asks his wife, Cassie, "On the last three days before you all leave on your trips, I have to get all your consent on paper and have it recorded at the courthouse to make it legal with the state laws of New Mexico, to capture all your brain waves and store them in a computer chip, along with you all's DNA."

Cassie responds, saying, "Sure, RJ. We will get it done. I love you so much, RJ."

RJ responds to Cassie, "I love you more than you ever can imagine, along with our wonderful kids. Let's make this a kids' week. What do you say, Cassie?"

"I would love it so very much, RJ. For all of us being together and having a barrel of fun, be wonderful for all of us. To feel loved. Thanks, RJ my love. Let's go for it," says Cassie.

RJ says, "Let's get the kids and let's go out for some pizza."

"Sounds great," Cassie says. Cassie asks RJ, "How about a movie?"

"Sure," says RJ. "I would like to share a story with you, Cassie, that I stumbled upon last year . . . and I meant to tell you about it, and I am going to tell you now. When you get to where you can have full access of your brain, you'll be able walk on water."

"Wow," Cassie says.

It's morning now, and it's time for Cassie and the kids to get ready to go on their flight overseas. RJ has all their luggage ready in the van. Now they are on their way to the airport. Everybody is feeling very excited and little sad 'cause Daddy is not coming this time. They get to the airport and go to have a healthy breakfast. After breakfast, it's time to separate and say their good-byes.

RJ got his eyes on the 777 jet liner taking off, waving at the 777 jet liner as it disappeared into the blue skies. RJ went straight to his labs and went right to work on his family's DNA and their memory brain waves and to have it recorded with different secret codes. It has to be programmed just right for it to work. RJ's works and his home project are getting to be a little too much for him. But he is very glad that he got a breathing machine helping him sleep a lot better. There's a time that RJ's mind goes into where he is able to use his whole mind instead just a portion of the whole human brain. There are times that RJ has to get off the breathing machine to be able to get more brilliant ideas that he needs for his project while he is just about near death with the sleep apnea that he's got. And he needs more brilliant ideas, information, to finish his project 99999 + 99999 = 1. And that's the only way RJ can get some brilliant idea from. RJ's been speaking to his family on the phone, and they are all doing well besides the kids missing their daddy a lot. They will be coming home soon. RJ can hardly wait to see them in human figure. RJ's family is very loving.

The two weeks are up, and RJ will be going to the airport at about 6:00 pm. RJ arrives early at the airport, when he heard that the jet where his family was aboard has just crashed in the sea.

RJ says, "Oh my god." RJ drops to his knees. He couldn't believe what he is seeing and hearing. No survivors on flight 2045. As he watches on the TV screen, news is coming, unfolding. RJ wouldn't accept that his whole family is gone. This is a big devastation to RJ. RJ is so glad that capturing his family's memories and their DNA through technology, nothing is impossible. He remembers when

RJ's wife came to his class. She was interested in learning how to operate the supercomputer and the codes. Now knowing that his whole family had deceased, RJ is so determined and very brilliant that he can bring back his family back alive with his project $99999 + 99999 = 1$. It may take up to six months to a year to bring his entire family back to life.

Learning how to use your whole brain is not easy. It's going to have to be programmed to be able to use it just right. Now you only allow to use a small portion of your brain. RJ Sumner wouldn't want to wait until he dies. Normally, you would have to wait until your life ended. And the deceased will have to wait for millions of years, for their reward after they're dead.

"Forget it," RJ says. "I got the technology right now and I am going to use it." RJ wants it right now while he is alive despite the difficulties of not being able to translate computer science with a normal mind. You need more brain power, like 100 percent. Learning computer science has helped many people including RJ. RJ names his project 99999 + 99999 = 1. RJ figures out everybody's reward that you will be receiving after you die. You are all going to be able to use your whole brain instead of just a small portion.

"When I get my family back, they will have the full capability of their whole brain." RJ gets his family code put into his specially made computer that he built to be able to bring his family back to life in case he ever have to. Now he's so glad he did learn computer science.

RJ is going through some hard times. RJ has to ask his boss for a two-month leave. RJ has a lot of work to do ahead of him.

Two months go by, and RJ is getting some response from his wife. It is making RJ feel so damn good all over again that he hasn't felt in such a long time. Happy and crying, RJ is so thankful that he got his family DNA and their DNA memory stored, jumping and hollering out loud all over the place when he heard that he could communicate with them through computer chips. But we all have the ability to make at least one tiny change. Now he's able to communicate with his whole family. RJ is so thankful that he's able to communicate with the whole family on the Internet although they are dead. Now he got his wife back through a computer chip where he can communicate with her and her beyond-brilliant brain that she's got now because of her death. That is the reward that you get afterward—have full capacity of your brain and being able to transmit to the supercomputer to reveal her identity. RJ invented. RJ Sumner wants to believe in himself and love himself again and can hardly wait to be able to feel his wife and kids. One touch from either one of them would feel so good right now. Now RJ is going to be able to get all the information that is needed from his wife to be able to put her DNA into the computer to have his wife's DNA analyzed. It might take about six months to a year for her DNA recipe to be completed and to install their memory into the computer that is receiving commands from his master and operating real very smoothly and to be able to get them back into human body. RJ now feels much better. RJ and his brilliant wife with a brain out of this universe. RJ is looking forward to that marvelous day, knowing that he's going to be together with his family again. RJ is going to make it happen. And all of his family will be created right inside his labs. It can cost RJ up to $300,000 to have one whole body back to life. It would be a huge breakthrough for the entire world if RJ the scientist created a way to bring the dead back to life, like his whole family having all their DNA stored. Now RJ has to follow all these rules randomly; you don't want to make it hard on yourself. Following all the codes is not impossible but possible; no, it's not hard but enough as it is. Following the codes he's needing and looking for them is not going to be that easy. You can't combine numbers in this case. Sensitivity and specificity codes have to be followed. This makes it very difficult for RJ to change the way anything works, under the statistical measures of this performance and classification testing. All this planning will take and consume time. Bringing back his family in human figure is a very complicated task but possible. But RJ needs to use all his intelligence and has to keep a special designer's code stored in a very special place in his gigantic computer. His secret code has its own language, and it's baffling if you're not used to it. It's almost like we have a secret code. For sure you have and have to reserve and respect his project $99999 + 99999 = 1$. In this business, everything has to be kept secret from the government. Right now all of RJ's energy is focused on bringing his family back alive and being with them again, like it used to be before. These measures come unsurprisingly from his wife, now that he's making contact with her through the computer pretty often, which he's enjoying a lot. She is the one with the intelligence now, which it needed badly on bringing her back alive, along with the kids. You see, RJ's wife has full capacity of her brain now—100 percent—because she is communicating from a computer chip although she's dead, without a human body, just her computer chip. In most cases, it is unlikely that any system will operate at full capacity for prolonged periods because of natural inefficiencies and other factors. But in this case, RJ has been communicating with his wife through a computer.

"Let's put it this way," RJ says, "it's like your brain's been cloned, but communicating through a computer chip. Communicating with the dead is how you would put it."

This was RJ's purpose in storing his whole family's brain's DNA. In case one of the events would ever take place, which it did, RJ would have to put his wife's DNA into stem cell tubes. The clear cell tube would have to be heated to the right temperature, with plenty of moisture. That is needed to start the process, and think about this creation and all the things that could go wrong. Any slight mistake you might make, you just might come up with a human very beautiful or very ugly. The reproduction process will be monitored very closely inside this large incubator that will be used for creating his family and can be crystallized in seconds. The female reproductive system allows for the necessary to nurture a fertilized egg to develop similar to a human fetus. It's going to be a very large egg that his family will be hatching out of. RJ Sumner the scientist will need monitoring of the stem cell tubes closely, about every four hours around the clock.

Three months went by, and everything is looking excellent. RJ feels so extraordinary and is picking momentum. Something's got a hold of RJ deep inside of him, and he's getting this feeling he's in motion. There's a sudden feeling of love that he's feeling all over his body. Now anytime the hatching will be taking place. RJ is supplied with everything. No need to worry, it's now. The hatching will take place naturally, which includes praying. Out of the experiences that RJ can honestly say was the best he ever invented was that RJ made it happen.

"Oh God, the hatching is taking place right now." His daughter is the first one to be hatched, and RJ is seeing everything happen.

He can't believe what is taking place. He is feeling so happy, noticing that he's going to need some clothing for them. Now his son is beginning to hatch, along with his son's mother. What a relief to the scientist it is. There's only one way that you can go about bringing back your family, and slim and one chance: by an opportunity given by the science facility. This method belongs to RJ, and all of his family's DNA had to have been recently stored.

It's the futuristic future. That will become a reality. In the near future, the world can use RJ's brilliant discovery. Thanks again for having sleep apnea. He is sure that with a beyond-brilliant family, they will accomplish the impossible. You'll have to watch your code processor on this as most code processors will try to undercode, will italicize the titles of project $99999 + 99999 = 1$. To complete this process, you must have access to your website source with code. For information on all the advanced configuration options, the first cheat codes are put in place for code testing purposes. Commentary codes can have the same effect because these are not games that you are playing with. You are dealing with an effort to make it all successful. This ingenious computer will have difficulty in finding codes that if you are not the master, you'll forget. RJ's family will find a cure for sleep apnea and conquer so many things. Do not try to capitalize codes when this title is acting as a description code following the codes to a successful enchantment.

Your Futuristic Future:
Project 99999 + 99999 = 1

The End